Contents

Transport

People use transport to get around. How much do **YOU** know about different forms of transport?

Cars

Some cars run on ice cream instead of petrol.

✗ **False!**

Most cars run on petrol.

Trains

Trains fly through the air to get from place to place.

✗ False!

Trains travel on the ground, not in the air! They move along special rails called railway tracks.

Buses

All buses have a roof.

✗ False!

Some buses do not have a roof. Tour buses do not have a roof. People ride in them to see the sights.

Planes

Planes have wings instead of wheels.

✔ **True or false?** ✗ 11

✗ **False!**

Planes have wings AND wheels.
Planes need their wheels for taking
off and landing.

Ships

Some boats move
using the wind.

 ✔ True or false? ✘

✓ **True!**

Some boats move using the wind.
They catch the wind with giant sails.

Bicycles

All bicycles have two wheels the same size.

 True or **false?**

✗ False!

This bike has one big wheel and one little wheel. It is called a penny-farthing!

Animals

Some people
use animals to
get around.

 True or false ?

17

✔ True!

Some people use animals to get around. Some horses pull people in carriages.

18

Balloons

Some people use balloons to fly from place to place.

✔ True!

Some people fly using giant hot air balloons. The people stand in a basket underneath the balloon.

Submarines

Some vehicles can travel under water.

✓ True!

Some vehicles can travel under water. These special boats are called submarines.

Can you remember?

Which vehicle has wheels and wings?

Which vehicle moves using the wind?

Which vehicle can travel under water?

Look back through the book to check your answers.

Index

Activity

Make your own True or False game

Help your child to make their own Transport: True or False game. Collect a selection of pictures of transport from magazines. Mount each picture on card. Then with the child write a series of true or false statements about the transport in the pictures on separate pieces of card. Put one statement with each corresponding picture. On the back of each picture write if the statement is true or false. For the game, read the statement out loud, ask the child if it is true or false, then turn over the picture to see if the child is correct. To extend the activity, ask the child to write the statements and whether they are true or false, and then ask you the questions.